Cooking with Max

45 Really Fun and Kind of Messy Recipes Kids Can Make

by Max Nania

With special tips and photography
by Sienna Nania

Little Five Star
A Division of
Five Star Publications, Inc.
Chandler, AZ

Linda F. Radke, President
Five Star Publications, Inc.
PO Box 6698
Chandler, AZ 85246-6698
480-940-8182
Website:www.CookingWithMax.com

Library of Congress Cataloging-in-Publication Data

Nania, Max.
  Cooking with Max : 45 really fun and kind of messy recipes kids can make / by Max Nania ; with special tips and photography by Sienna Nania.
     p. cm.
  ISBN-13: 978-1-58985-059-0
  ISBN-10: 1-58985-059-9
  1. Cookery--Juvenile literature. I. Nania, Sienna. II. Title.
  TX652.5.N354 2007
  641.5'123--dc22

                         2006101802

Printed in Canada

Editor: Laura L. Ahrens
Project Manager: Sue DeFabis
Cover & Interior Design: Linda Longmire
Cooking Tips & Photography: Sienna Nania

Cooking With Max

Dedication

I dedicate this book to my grandmas—Grandma Elaine, who taught my mom how to cook and Grandma Lena, who I cook for every Thanksgiving!

Max Nania

I dedicate this book to my dear husband John. He has at least tried everything we ever created in the kitchen, proving that he's both supportive and brave!

Sienna Nania

Max and I would like to thank the great team at Five Star Publications for all of their support and help. We would also like to thank our wonderful editor, Laura Ahrens and our dear aunt, Darby Lofstrand, who inspired us to publish the book in the first place. Darby, you're the best!

Cooking With Max

Table of Contents

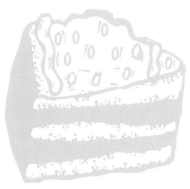

Tips for Grown-ups from Max's Mom

Mom's Tips

Hello! I am Sienna, Max's mom. I love the kitchen and I really love using the kitchen as a classroom. The time you and your child spend cooking together creates not only wonderful memories but great opportunities for learning, as well. My family and I talk in the kitchen, create in the kitchen, eat in the kitchen, and have fun in the kitchen.

Max started cooking with me when he was a baby in his high chair. He learned to count by sorting out Goldfish and Cheerios to mix together for his Bubbles and Fish recipe. He learned his colors by naming the colors of the food we were working with, like yellow bananas or red apples. In fact, this whole cookbook came about because Max needed some work on his handwriting. Our creative solution was to write down the things we invented in the kitchen for a family cookbook. This eventually became the book you are reading now.

I hope you enjoy Max's book and that it inspires you to enjoy some time with a child in the heart of every home - the kitchen. Don't worry if you are not a cook. Remember, your child doesn't know that and besides, these recipes were developed by a little boy who still needs reminders for which shoe goes on what foot!

Fear not! Make a mess and have fun.

Ten tips to get you started and to help save your sanity:

1. Take a few minutes to get everything set up before your little cook gets in there.
2. Read the recipe and make sure you have everything you need.
3. Make sure your cooking spot is easy for little hands to get to. If the counter is too high, try stirring the soup on the kitchen table and then take it over to the stove.
4. Know that kids are going to taste things, so set out a tasting spoon and be prepared to wash hands more than once.
5. Read the recipe with your little cooks before you start so they know what is going on. Go over the order in which you will be doing things. This helps with their listening skills.
6. Explain the rules of the kitchen. Make sure they know which tools are theirs and which tools (stove) are for the grown-up helper.
7. Use aprons! They're fun to dress-up in and cut down on laundry. Tie back hair or have a cooking hat to keep hair on the head and not in the food.
8. Be brave and let your kids experiment. Max thought a pickle and peanut butter Oreo-type snack would be good. I'll admit it looked really cool, but it sure didn't make the book.
9. Remember, the final product doesn't need to look like it came from a Food Network special. What matters is that it's fun and tasty!
10. And hey, life is messy. Just clean it up and make sure the kids help.

Max's Tips for Kids

Hi! My name is Max. I'm seven years old, and I've been cooking my whole life. You know what? Cooking is fun! You should try it. I think you might really get into it and want to cook and learn about food your whole life, too.

I hope you like the recipes that my mom and I made up.

Grown-ups make really good helpers. Among other things, they can do jobs that are too hard for kids and they can do things that might hurt us kids if we tried to do them by ourselves.

Max

Here are 10 tips for cooking with grown-ups:

1. Never put anything on the stove by yourself. *(This is definitely a job for your grown-up helper.)* This goes for putting things in the oven, too.
2. If you're under five years old, only cut with a plastic knife. If you're older than five, you can use a butter knife.
3. Let your grown-up helper chop up food with the sharp knives.
4. Be sure to help clean up after you are done cooking or baking.
5. Be nice to your little brothers and sisters when they're cooking, because little kids make lots of mistakes. My little brother's name is Ian and he can really be messy!
6. If you make a mess, blame it on your little brother or sister. *(Okay, Mom, this was just a joke!)*
7. Check your ingredients to make sure you have enough of the right stuff before you start mixing them together.
8. Reading is cool. Read the recipe *(and check out my list of books that go with them).* I read a recipe at least a couple of times before I get started.
9. If you make a mistake, it's okay. Just tell your grown-up helper.
10. Ask your grown-up helper to cook more with you. Invite your friends to cook with you, too. My friends and I make stuff together in the kitchen all the time. That is the funnest part.

cookie cutter cheese

Always a hit at class parties.

Max Says:

"Hey, kids, cheese is good. My Grandma and Grandpa O. are from Wisconsin. These people know cheese."

Ingredients & Utensils

- 2 to 3 slices of cheese *(deli slices of provolone and sharp cheddar work really well.)*
- 20 to 30 crackers *(we use whole wheat saltines for squares and water crackers for circles.)*
- cookie cutters *(the little ones.)*

Directions:

Arrange some crackers on a plate. Place slices of cheese on a cutting board and use the cookie cutters on them. Put the cheese shapes on the crackers and serve.

Mom's Tips

We use reindeer and bell cookie cutters for Christmas, and stars and moons cookie cutters for Halloween. Sometimes, we use hummus or cream cheese as a spread and a tomato under the cheese just to make it extra fancy. Suggested reading: *Frederick* by Loe Leo Lionni *(One of our favorite mice.)*

dipping chip stars
more fun with cookie cutters.

Ingredients & Utensils

- 4 or 5 10-inch flour tortillas
- 1 10-16 oz. bag of blue corn chips
- 1 bowl of favorite dip *(Mom and I like mild salsa.)*
- cookie sheet *(dark ones work best but the shiny ones work too.)*
- olive oil
- salt
- star-shaped cookie cutter
- cutting board

"I like this treat when I am studying the planets."

Max and Cafe Chef Keith Schockling cooking together at Wolfgang Puck's Cafe in Orlando Florida.

Directions:

Place a flour tortilla on a cutting board and use the cookie cutter to cut out star shapes. Place the stars on the cookie sheet. Spray them with olive oil, and sprinkle with a pinch of salt. Have your grown-up helper preheat the oven to 350 degrees, and then bake your Dipping Chip Stars for 5 minutes or until the edges get a little brown. Not all tortillas are created the same, so watch them. Have your grown-up helper take them out of the oven. Let them cool and then dump them into a basket with the blue corn chips. It looks like a sky of chips. Cool, eh?

Try different shapes for different occasions. A heart cookie cutter works well with red chips for Valentines day.
Suggested reading: *The Magic School Bus: Lost in the Solar System*, by Joanna Cole and Bruce Degen *(Or any cool space book.)*

Mom's tips

bubbles and fish

Great for stroller walks or hiking.

Max says:

"This was
my first recipe
ever."

Ingredients & Utensils

- 1 cup of Goldfish crackers
- 1 cup of Cheerios
- 1 to 2 oz. size of M&M's
- 1.5 oz. box of raisins
- 1 green fruit roll-up (optional)
- 1 medium-sized bowl
- 1 spoon

Directions:

Okay, here's what you do. Pour the ingredients into the bowl. Then stir gently with a big spoon. Eat 'em right away or put them into a bag for your walk.

Mom's tips

If you're going to eat this at home, try serving it in a little plastic fishbowl! Add two more small bags of M&M's to the bottom to look like gravel. You can put a green fruit roll-up "plant" on the wall of the fishbowl to make it look even more fun. Suggested reading: *The Rainbow Fish* by Marcus Pfister or *The Cheerios Animal Play Book* by Lee Wade *(Great for the littlest cooks.)*

cinco de mayo oranges

Not just for May 5th.

Ingredients & Utensils ➤

- one orange
- cinnamon
- powdered sugar

Directions:
Even the littlest of cooks can peel the oranges. Then have the grown-up helper cut them into circles. Sprinkle with cinnamon and powdered sugar.

Max Says:

"Hey kids, this is a good snack. It's easier than making cereal and milk."

This great treat is straight from the Mexican marketplace. Why not try counting the orange circles in Spanish? Show the kids a map of Mexico. For a field trip, visit a farmers market. Explain that these treats are often served in Mexican markets. Suggested reading: Find an Atlas. The kids will love the maps. Have them find home and Mexico.

Mom's Tips

11

bread sticks

A great afternoon snack on cold rainy days.

Max Says:

"These are fun to make with friends! My friend Jordan and I make these when we eat pizza."

Ingredients & Utensils

- 1 can of refrigerator biscuits
- Lawry's seasoned salt
- parmesan cheese
- red pasta sauce
- cookie sheet
- aluminum foil

Directions:

Have your grown-up helper preheat the oven to 400 degrees. Next, have your grown-up helper pop open the can of biscuits. Using the aluminum foil, make a tray and shake some seasoned salt and parmesan cheese in it (just enough to cover the bottom). Next, stretch the biscuits into fat little sticks and roll them in the salt and cheese. Place on the cookie sheet. Have your grown-up helper put the cookie sheet in the oven and bake for 8 to 12 minutes or until golden. Serve with red sauce to dip 'em in.

Mom's tips

These bread sticks are fun and easy for kids to make. Max makes them while I'm getting the soup, spaghetti, or pizza ready for dinner. We like to serve them with olive oil and fresh herbs. Suggested reading: *Cloudy with a Chance of Meatballs* by Judi Barrett, Illustrated by Ron Barret.

even better biscuits

Because Max thought regular biscuits were boring.

Ingredients & Utensils

- 2¼ cups of biscuit mix
- ⅔ cups of milk
- 1 tbsp. fresh rosemary
  (my mom grows it outside.)
- or 2 tsp. dried rosemary *(if you don't have fresh.)*
- 2 handfuls of your favorite shredded
- cheese *(I like parmesan and mild cheddar.)*
- 1 large bowl
- 1 wood spoon
- baking sheet
- olive oil

Max Says:

"These are good with soup! Cheese in bread is a great idea."

Directions:

Mix all the ingredients together except the olive oil. Spray the baking sheet with the olive oil so you can get the biscuits off when they're done. With the wood spoon, plop down little piles of biscuits. Then have your grown-up helper bake them in an oven at 450 degrees for 8 to 10 minutes.

You can also add chopped olives for an extra special taste sensation. Suggested reading: *What Do People Do All Day?* by Richard Scarry. Or at the library find the bread section. Read about the role bread has played in feeding people throughout the ages.

Mom's Tips

oh yeah! fruit salad

Side dish or dessert.

"Like the song says, Fruit Salad yummy, yummy!"

Ingredients & Utensils

- 1 banana
- 1 8-oz. can of pineapple *(Fresh pineapple won't work. It is too difficult for kids to cut and work with.)*
- 1 cup seedless grapes - you pick the color
- ½ cup shredded coconut
- handful of nuts - your choice (we like almond slivers or walnuts or honey roasted peanuts.)
- 1 mystery fruit *(time to try something new — Max says you can't go wrong with any fruit the color of orange, such as mangos, mandarin orange slices, etc.)*
- 2 tablespoons of honey
- 1 large mixing bowl
- 1 big spoon
- chopping board
- plastic knife *(one for each kid who's helping you.)*

Directions:

Get a pretty big bowl. Use a plastic knife to chop up your "mystery" fruit and then put the fruit in the bowl. Stir your fruit together. Finally sprinkle on your honey and coconut and nuts. Put the juice from the canned pineapple into your salad if you would like some fruit dressing. Enjoy!

Mom's tips

I love fruit salad because it can be a group activity. Have one child chop one fruit while another child crushes the nuts in a plastic bag. Calling it "Mystery Fruit" is not only funny, it's an excellent way to get your family to try new fruits and berries. Have your little cooks guess where in the world the different fruits come from. Check out a world map to see how international your fruit salad is. We added kiwis one time and hit five continents. Suggested reading: *The Owl and the Pussycat* by Edward Lear, Illustrated by Jan Brett. Ah, slices of quince.

cinnamon toast popcorn

So good and no fat from butter.

Max Says:

"It is a really good sprinkley treat for Friday night movie night."

Ingredients & Utensils

- 1 bowl of freshly popped popcorn
- ¼ cup of powdered sugar
- 1 tbsp. of cinnamon
- ⅓ cup of slivered almonds
- 1 large bowl

Directions:

Put your hot popped popcorn in the bowl. In a cup, stir together your cinnamon and powdered sugar. Then spoon mixture over the top of popcorn and gently shake the bowl. Sprinkle almonds on top.

Mom's tips

We use a hot air popper to make our popcorn. It's fun and healthy for you and the kids. Also, you can use regular sugar, but powdered sugar will stick to the popcorn better. Suggested reading: *Sock Monkey Goes to Hollywood: A Star is Bathed* by Cece Bell.

dad's seasoned popcorn

A savory treat

Max Says:

"This is salty
and delicious
at the
same time."

Ingredients & Utensils

- 1 bowl of freshly popped popcorn
- seasoned salt (we use Lawry's.)
- parmesan cheese
- 1 large bowl

Directions:

This one is so simple. Shake seasoned salt and sprinkle a little parmesan cheese on top of a hot bowl of popcorn. Could it be any easier?

Mom's tips

Popcorn add-ins are fun and they let the kids feel like they are really creating. Here are a few of our favorites: crushed candy canes, raisins, M&M's, Cracker Jacks, dried apricots and powdered sugar mixed with pumpkin pie spice. Suggested Reading: *The Popcorn Book* by Tomie de Paola. Read *Sock Monkey* again. It is that fun!

spinach poofs

You will love spinach! Really...

"Spinach is good for you and these taste great."

Ingredients & Utensils

- 1 can of crescent rolls
- 1 can of spinach or 1 package of frozen spinach
- 1/4 cup olive oil
- 1 small onion
- 1/2 cup of finely ground almonds
- 1/4 cup of shredded parmesan cheese
- black pepper
- 2-cup measuring cup
- spoon
- cookie sheet

Directions:

First, you gotta squeeze the juice out of the spinach (do this over the sink). Then put the spinach aside. Next, put the olive oil in your 2-cup measuring cup and add the almonds. By now, your mixture should be at the 3/4 cup mark. Now add the cheese. Where does the mixture come to now on the cup? Next, use your spoon to mix in the spinach and chopped onion and set it aside. Now pop open the crescent rolls. Fill the rolls by putting a spoonful of the spinach mixture at the bottom of each triangular piece of dough and roll them up as you normally would. Place them on the cookie sheet and have your grown-up helper bake them according to the crescent roll directions on the can.

Sprinkle the tops of the rolls with extra parmesan. This is a sneaky but tasty way to get spinach into your family's diet. We sometimes serve these with scrambled eggs for breakfast. Suggested reading: *The Tale of Peter Rabbit* by Beatrix Potter.

Mom's tips

corny cornbread

A Fall Favorite.

Ingredients & Utensils

- 1 box of corn bread mix
- $\frac{1}{3}$ cup of sour cream
- 1 cup fresh corn *(canned works too.)*
- 1 tbsp. milk
- olive oil spray

Max Says:

"It's corntacular!
Shuck corn
outside because
it can get
all over
your house."

Directions:

Put all the ingredients into a big bowl and stir just until mixed. Then, spray a pie tin with olive oil and then spoon the mixture in. Have your grown-up helper put it in the oven set at 400 degrees for 15 to 20 minutes or until golden brown on top. Take out and let cool a few minutes before you cut it like a pie.

Mom's Tips

Max is right about shucking corn outside to reduce mess. If anyone likes spicy food, you can always add crushed red peppers to the mix. Suggested reading: *Turk and Runt* by Lisa Wheeler, Illustrated by Frank Ansley. Very Funny!

Cooking With Max

thanksgiving cranberries

Or anytime cranberries.

Max Says:

Ingredients & Utensils

- 1 can of whole berry cranberry jelly
- nutmeg
- cinnamon
- ground cloves
- 1 cup of walnut pieces
- 1 large mixing bowl

"We use these all the time. They go perfect with cornbread. I make these with Grandma Lena."

Directions:

In a bowl, dump out the cranberries and chop them up so they aren't in the shape of the can anymore. Next, add a dash of nutmeg and cinnamon and some ground cloves. Add the walnuts and stir. Serve them hot by microwaving for 30 seconds (or just serve them at regular room temperature). It looks like you spent hours on them.

Mom's Tips

This little project is a good one to do just before you serve Thanksgiving dinner. It's a great idea for keeping the kids out of your way while you put everything on the table. Beware - cranberries stain. Aprons are always a good idea. Placemats help, too. Suggested reading: *I Am the Turkey* by Michele Sobel Spirn, Illustrated by Joy Allen.

groovy green beans

Eat your green veggies and like it.

Max Says:

Ingredients & Utensils

- 1 14 oz. can of green beans *(fresh works great, too.)*
- 3 tbsp. of soy sauce
- handful of almond slices
- 1 large mixing bowl

"This one was inspired by Chinese take-out food. It's green, delicious, and good for you."

Directions:

Have your grown-up helper cook the beans for you and put them in a bowl. Next, mix in the soy sauce and then top it all off with the almond slices (one of those small, 1-ounce bags is usually enough). Serve.

Mom's tips

This is a nice alternative to butter and the can of mushroom soup traditionally used on green beans. Suggested reading: *The Five Chinese Brothers* by Claire Huchet Bishop and Kurt Weise or *Zen Shorts* by Jon J. Muth.

apple salad

This is great in the Fall or for a back to school dinner.

Ingredients & Utensils

- 2 Red Delicious apples
- 4 oz. vanilla yogurt
- 1/2 cup walnut pieces
- 1 small box of raisins *(approx. 1/3 cup.)*
- 1 handful of dried cranberries or golden raisins
- 3 dashes of cinnamon
- bowl
- butter knife
- cutting board

Max Says:

"This is our favorite September salad! I invented it after making prints with paint and apples in school when I was little. Yogurt tastes better than the mayonnaise."

Directions:

Okay, first have your grown-up helper slice the apples with a big knife. You can have them then cut them up into triangles — or if you are old enough, you can do it. Next put everything in the bowl, except the yogurt and cinnamon. Stir it up. Now add the yogurt and stir again. Next add the cinnamon and stir some more until it's all coated. Ta Da! Apple salad!

This salad can be doubled or halved depending on how much you need to serve. Have the children figure out how much more or less you need to make it. Apples are popular in school in the fall. You can have a tasting contest with yellow, green, and red apples and see if the kids can tell the difference without looking. Then decide which ones will go into your dish. Suggested reading: *Ten Apples Up on Top* by Dr. Seuss (Theodor Seuss Geisel)

Mom's tips

Max's best peanut butter

Peanut butter from scratch is fun!

Max Says:

"This is great
in the
Tarzan Wrap."

Ingredients & Utensils

- 1 cup of honey roasted peanuts
- 1/2 cup of dry roasted peanuts
- 2 tbsp. olive oil
- 1/2 cup milk chocolate chips
- blender
- 1 wood spoon
- 1 airtight container

Directions:

Place all the ingredients in the blender that your grown-up helper has set up for you. Now make sure the lid is on. Have your grown-up helper press the blender's "chop" button (your grown-up helper might let you if you're old enough — but you have to ask first!) When the nuts all go to the side, stop and use the wooden spoon to push the mixture back to the middle. Once you're sure the lid is back on tightly, press the "chop" button — or try the other buttons. Repeat this whole process as many times as necessary until it looks like peanut butter. It takes a while!
WARNING: *Never put your hand in the blender and always let your grown-up helper clean it up for you. The blades on the bottom are way sharp and can really hurt, so always have some help.*

Mom's tips

Be patient. Blending can take a while. It is worth the wait. Suggested reading: *The Life and Times of the Peanut* by Charles Micucci.

Cooking With Max

peanut butter dip

Mmmm, good.

Ingredients & Utensils

- 1/2 cup of peanut butter
- 1/2 cup of cream cheese
- several carrot sticks
- 1 apple (sliced)
- 1 large mixing bowl
- 1 large plate

Max Says:

"This dip really tastes good. So try this snack because it is good for you. Moms and Dads might like it, too."

Directions:

In a mixing bowl, combine the two ingredients and stir until they're blended together. Plop the whole mixture in the center of a plate, and place carrot sticks and apple slices all around it like the sun.

Ask the kids to name the three food groups that are in this snack. What would this taste good on (for example, whole wheat toast)? Take your kids to the public library and find a book about peanuts. Did you know peanuts aren't nuts? Suggested reading: *Stuart's Cape* by Sara Pennypacker, Illustrated by Martin Matje.

Mom's Tips

veggie lemon butter

Because sometimes veggies need a sidekick.

Max Says:

"By using good
sauces I can
make my veggies
disappear."

Ingredients & Utensils

- 1 large lemon
- 2 tbsp. of butter
- veggie of choice *(this tastes awesome on carrots, broccoli, asparagus, peas, and green beans.)*
- 1 microwave-safe cup

Directions:

Put the butter in the cup. Next, roll the lemon back and forth on the table and press down on it while you sing the ABC's. Why? Because this is just long enough to make the juice come out of the lemon easier. Have your grown-up helper slice the lemon in half. Now squeeze the lemon juice over the butter in the cup. Have your grown-up helper microwave it for 20 seconds. Stir it up and pour on top of cooked veggies.

Mom's Tips

I have found that getting the kids involved in making the veggies helps in getting the kids to try the veggies. Why not check out the food pyramid in the back of the book and show them how important eating veggies are for a kid. Suggested reading: *How Do Dinosaurs Eat Their Food?* by Jane Yolen, Illustrated by Mark Teague.

veggies-be-gone sauce

Because sometimes veggies need some extra yumm...

Max Says:

"Cheese is from the dairy group. In this recipe you get food from both the dairy and vegetable groups."

Ingredients & Utensils

- 1 16 oz. jar of cheese sauce
- 4 oz. of salsa
- veggie of choice (*I like baked potatoes and broccoli.*)
- pepper
- 1 microwave-safe bowl

Directions:

Empty jar of cheese sauce into bowl. Stir in **salsa** and add a dash of pepper. Have your grown-up helper put the bowl in the microwave for one minute. Stir again. If it's not warm all the way through, microwave for another 15 seconds.

This can also be a dip for chips. Suggested reading: *I'm Still Here in the Bathtub* by Alan Katz, Illustrated by David Catrow.

Mom's tips

honey better

Sweet and better for you.

Ingredients & Utensils ⟾

- 4 tbsp. olive oil buttery spread
- 1 tbsp. honey
- 1 cup or small bowl

Directions:

In the cup, mush the two ingredients up until well blended. Serve in the cup or scoop it out onto a pretty plate.

"I call it this because it is better for you than butter. It's good for Grandpa's cholesterol, so it will be good for you, too."

Mom's Tips

My family has cholesterol problems big time, so we use a lot of olive oil in our cooking. You can substitute olive oil or olive oil spread (like margarine) in many of your favorite dishes for a healthier you. Recommended reading: An excellent time to read any of the *Winnie the Pooh* books by A.A. Milne!

cool stuff with cocoa

Or maybe you call it hot chocolate

Ingredients & Utensils

- 1 cup of milk
- 1 to 2 Tablespoons of chocolate syrup *(How much chocolate can you handle?)*
- 1 or 2 big marshmallows
- rolling pin
- cutting board
- cookie cutters (*I like to use a little ghost one.*)

Directions:

Have your grown-up helper microwave a cup of milk for one minute then add the chocolate syrup to taste. While your grown-up helper is doing that, you can use a rolling pin to smoosh your marshmallows down onto the cutting board. Then use your cookie cutter on them (you can use a plastic knife if you don't have a cookie cutter) to cut out the shape of a ghost. I like to poke holes for eyes. When your hot chocolate is ready to drink, float your marshmallow ghost on top. Enjoy.

Instead of chocolate syrup, I sometimes use a packet of cocoa and mix it with half milk and half water. This recipe is really cute in the winter. Instead of a ghost, we use a bell or star cut out and a candy cane reindeer. By the way, to keep the marshmallows from sticking to the cutting board, dust it first with powdered sugar. Suggested reading: *The Polar Express* by Chris Van Allsburg.

Mom's tips

georgia lemonade

A new southern drink for summer.

Max Says:

"You don't have
to live in Georgia
to drink this."

Ingredients & Utensils 🍴

- 1 11-12 oz. can of peach nectar
- 1 12 oz. can of frozen lemonade
- 1 fuzzy, juicy peach
- pitcher

Directions:

Cut the peach into slices and put them in the freezer until they're frozen solid. Next, put your frozen lemonade in a pitcher and add your can of peach nectar. Then add water according the directions on the frozen lemonade. Now use the frozen peach slices instead of ice so your lemonade won't get watery. Yummy!

Mom's Tips

Instead of peaches, try frozen strawberries, too. Help the kids make a lemonade stand, even if it is just for the family. A fun educational opportunity with this recipe is to find Georgia on the map and talk about your own state. Suggested reading: *My First Atlas* by Bill Boyle.

Cooking With Max

super sport slushy

I thought of this on a really hot 4th of July

"Hey Kids!
Snow cones
and slushies are
full of sugar
and syrup.
These taste
just as good."

Ingredients & Utensils

- 12 oz. of blue sports drink
- 12 oz. of red sports drink
- blender
- ice *(filled to top of blender)*
- 2 gallon-size ziplock bags

Directions:

Pour 12 oz. of blue sports drink into blender and fill the rest with ice. Blend away! Push ALL the buttons! When all the ice is chopped up, stop! Have your grown-up helper pour it into the ziplock bag. Repeat this process with your red sports drink. You can store this in your freezer or cooler until you serve it. When you serve it, snip one of the lower corners of the blue ziplock bag and squeeze the slushy into your glass until half full. Then snip your red bag and squeeze that slushy on top of the blue slushy in your glass. Add a white straw, and you have a red, white and blue slushy!

Blender Safety: Only grown-ups operate blenders. Only spoons go inside the blender with the food — NEVER your fingers! No button pushing when lid is off. Really. No, really! Only grown-ups are allowed to clean the unplugged blender. Suggested reading: *Max the Minnow* by William Boniface, Illustrated by Don Sullivan. Because Max gets healthy.

Mom's tips

spritzers

Ooooooh, Spritzers!

Max Says:

"They are
sooo fizzy they
explode with
flavor in your
mouth."

Ingredients & Utensils

- 6 oz. apple juice
- 6 oz. lemon lime soda or ginger ale
- ½ glass ice
- 2 apple slices per glass
- 1 12-oz. glass

Directions:

Fill your glass with ice and toss in a couple of apple slices. Fill glass halfway with the apple juice, and then fill it the rest of the way up with the soda.

Mom's tips

Don't put these in sippy cups, as they tend to blow their lids! For variety, try other fruit juices. These go great with popcorn during sleepovers or for an afternoon snack. We use them whenever we have something to celebrate!
Suggested reading: We All Fall for Apples by Emmi S. Herman

afternoon tea

Comforting.

Max Says:

"This is good anytime, but it's REALLY good if you are sick."

Ingredients & Utensils 🍴

- ¾ cup Tang
- ½ cup iced tea mix
- 1 .13-.23 oz. packet of lemonade mix
  (the kind without sugar in it.)
- 1 tbsp. of cinnamon
- pinch of cloves
- 1 large mixing bowl

Directions:

Combine all of the ingredients in the mixing bowl and stir gently. Store in an airtight container. For tea, mix a heaping spoonful of your mixture into a cup of very warm water. *(Mom and I use a microwave, but you could use a kettle, too.)* Enjoy!

This is a good recipe to use when discussing the difference between mixtures and solutions. The dry ingredients are a mixture, but when you add the water, it turns into a solution. This is great tea full of vitamin C! Read some *Paddington Bear* books by Michael Bond.

Mom's tips

kid's chocolate baguette

Ooh la la!

"Moms beware –
powdered sugar
makes a mess.
But these are
really good."

Ingredients & Utensils 🍴

- 1 can of refrigerator biscuits
- 8 Hershey Kisses *(or the same as the number of biscuits.)*
- ½ cup powdered sugar
- 1 cookie sheet

Directions:

Have your grown-up helper pop open the can of biscuits. Take a biscuit and put a Hershey's Kiss in the middle. Then pull the dough over the chocolate so you can't see it anymore. Put them on an ungreased cookie sheet.

Have your grown-up helper put them in the oven and let them bake at 400 degrees for 10 to 12 minutes or until golden. Let your grown-up helper take them out of the oven. Wait at least 2 minutes and then dust them with the powdered sugar (to reduce mess, put the powdered sugar in a salt shaker). Eat them warm.

Mom's tips

A baguette is a thin loaf of French bread. You can use this Kid's Baguette to talk about France. Tell your kids that in France, Bastille Day (similar to our Independence Day) is celebrated each year on July 14. Show them on a map where France is located. Read a French children's story like *Madeleine*, written and illustrated by Ludwig Bemelmans. Suggested reading: *Madeleine* by Ludwig Bemelmans.

extra eggs
Sunday Brunch Regular.

Max Says:

"Extra eggs because I always ask for extra."

Ingredients & Utensils

- 6 eggs
- ½ cup shredded cheese
- seasoned salt
- fresh basil
- rosemary

Directions:

The kids can mix up all the ingredients in the bowl and add three dashes of seasoned salt. Then let the grown-up helper cook it in a skillet on the stove.

If your home is anything like ours, this will become a regular Sunday brunch dish for your family, too. Suggested reading: *Green Eggs and Ham* by Dr. Seuss *(Hey, a few drops of green food coloring and you too, can have green eggs.)*

Mom's tips

breakfast sundaes

Fun to do on April Fools Day.

Max Says:

"This one's great for April Fools Day! Add any kind of fruit. It will be quite excellent."

Ingredients & Utensils

- 1 banana
- 1 container of yogurt with fruit on the bottom
- 1 can whipped cream *(Max calls it "zyuhuz".)*
- sprinkles
- graham crackers or granola

Directions:

Okay, first you slice the banana and put it in the bottom of your bowl. Then you plop out the yogurt on top so that its 'fruit on the bottom' is on top (it'll look like ice cream topping). Last but not least, you add the whipped cream and sprinkles. Fun and good for you!

Mom's tips

So it's whipped cream for breakfast, you say? Well, I read the can and with the sprinkles, it only adds 10 calories to your meal. This is a fun and extra special breakfast that covers a lot of the food groups. Hey, have you checked out the latest food pyramid? I told my kids that yogurt is a cousin of ice cream. Suggested reading: *Fancy Nancy* by Jane O'Connor and Robin Preiss Glasser.

Cooking With Max

tie-dyed pancakes

A weekend tradition at the Nania home.

Max Says:

"These are crazy and flipping is fun!"

Ingredients & Utensils

- 2 cups of pancake mix
- 1/3 cup of milk
- 1/3 cup of sour cream
- 1 egg
- 1 tbsp. of cinnamon
- 1 tbsp. of vanilla
- food coloring
- large bowl
- 3 cups (like coffee cups or teacups.)

Directions:

In a large bowl, combine all the ingredients except the food coloring. Stir them all together until just a few lumps can be seen. Then, pour a little of this pancake batter into your three cups. In each cup, put a drop or two of your food coloring in and then stir. You now have 3 cups and 1 bowl of pancake batter.

Use the uncolored batter to make your main pancake by pouring it first into the pan. Next, put a little spoon of each colored batter on top of the pancake batter in the pan. Then swirl it all around with a spoon. There you have it —tie-dyed pancakes! Have your grown-up helper flip and cook them as usual.

Before you begin, you might consider reading *Pancakes, Pancakes* by Eric Carle. See how much fun you can have making pancakes. And the FLIPPING! Flipping is fun and I've had 30 some years of practice, so I can flip from the stove to the table. Children, however, should not attempt this, as the pan is hot. Let them learn how to do it after the meal by using a cold pan and leftover pancakes. That's how you learn in my house. Suggested reading: *If You Give a Pig a Pancake* by Laura Numeroff, Illustrated by Felicia Bond.

Mom's tips

tarzan wraps

Great afternoon snack or lunch box treat.

Max Says:

"I put chocolate sauce or honey on these sometimes."

Ingredients & Utensils

- One whole wheat tortilla
- peanut butter *(enough to cover your tortilla.)*
- 1 teaspoon sunflower seeds
- 1 banana

Directions:

Spread the peanut butter on the tortilla and sprinkle a few sunflower seeds on it. Next, cut up the banana and place on the tortilla. Now carefully roll it up. Enjoy!

Mom's Tips

Even the littlest cooks can cut bananas by using a plastic child's knife. Place the wrap on the plate seam side down to help it hold together. You can cut the wrap into circles for a snack. Suggested reading: *Eight Silly Monkeys* - by Steve Haskamp.

pizza soup

A fast weekday meal.

Ingredients & Utensils ✐

- 1 jar (1 lb 10 oz.) of organic spaghetti sauce
- 1 16 oz. can of veggie stock or 2 cups of milk
- ½ cup shredded pizza cheese *(to garnish the top.)*
- 1 dozen water crackers
- 1 soup pot

"This is a good dinner to have in the summer. I put fresh rosemary on top of each bowl to look cool."

Directions:

Combine spaghetti sauce and milk (or veggie stock) in a soup pot. Then have your grown-up helper heat it up on the stove while stirring often. Once warmed, serve in bowls with shredded cheese on top and those circle water crackers on the side. Ta da — Pizza Soup!

This is a tasty and conveniently fast weekday meal. It goes great with bread sticks. Max doesn't particularly care for tomatoes, but he loves pizza. So we came up with Pizza Soup. Do you have a picky eater in your house? Try changing the name of your dish! Suggested reading: *The Laughing Dragon* by Kenneth Mahood. The dragon makes hot soup.

Mom's Tips

pumpkin patch soup

My favorite fall soup.

Ingredients & Utensils

- 1 15 oz. can of pumpkin
- 1 16 oz. can of veggie broth
- 1 16 oz. can of black beans
- pinch of nutmeg
- 1 teaspoon of cinnamon
- ½ cup sour cream
- dash of hot sauce or a little crushed red pepper *(optional.)*
- 1 soup pot

Max Says:

"It has super foods in it to make you strong."

Directions:

This is so simple! Take your soup pot and plop in the pumpkin and black beans. Next, stir in the veggie broth. Add the pumpkin spices (nutmeg and cinnamon). Stir like crazy, and then give it to your grown-up helper to cook over medium heat on the stove. Tell them to stir it once in a while, too. Serve when hot with a dab of sour cream on top. To spice things up, we put a dash of hot sauce in my mom's soup and crushed red pepper in my dad's.

Mom's tips

You can mix everything up at the table and then move it to the stove. This helps keep little ones well away from the stove. Max was trying to combine two of his favorites–black beans and pumpkin pie–and it worked. I personally like this over cheese ravioli. Max wasn't a fan of it, but I thought it was awesome! Suggested reading: *Pumpkin Town* by Katie McKy illustrated by Pablo Bernasconi.

pirate pasta

Golden carrot coins! Pea pearls. ARGGG! It is good, mateys!

Ingredients & Utensils

- 1 package of frozen cheese mini-raviolis

- 1 cup frozen peas

- 4 big or 2 cups carrots cut into circles *or* frozen carrot coins steamed or cooked until tender.

- 4 Tablespoons veggie lemon butter *(See recipe on page 24)*

- fresh basil
- rosemary
- 1 large pot

"Find the best bowl you have and the greatest ingredients you have and you will have a great ARGGG in the bowl."

Directions:

Put peas (and carrots, too, if they're frozen) in the pot and have an adult put it on the stove and bring to a boil. Once boiling, have your grown-up helper add the pasta and cook as directed. Drain and dump into a bowl. Once your grown-up helper has done that, you can mix in all the rest of the ingredients and serve.

Mom's tips

Try adding parmesan cheese and ruby red tomatoes. A good story to read while your Pirate Pasta is cooking is *Pirate Pup* by Caroline Stutson and Robert Rayevsky or any good pirate tale! Suggested reading: *Jack Sparrow: The Siren Song* by Rob Kidd. A chapter book Max loved.

shapes for lunch

The kitchen as your classroom.

Max Says:

"Here is one for the baby brothers and sisters learning their shapes."

Ingredients & Utensils

- 1 hard-boiled egg
- 4 whole wheat saltine crackers
- 1 slice of cheese
- 1 handful seedless green grapes
- 1 handful blue corn tortilla chips
- 1 apple sliced
- 1 large plate

Directions:

Slice the egg into circles and the cheese into rectangles. You can slice the grapes in half the long way to make ovals and apple slices are ready-made crescents or moon shapes! Put these on the plate along with the square crackers and the triangle-shaped blue corn tortilla chips. That's all there is to it!

Mom's tips

This recipe of Max's is a great way to help your children learn while they're eating healthy food. The game I played with Max and his baby brother Ian (who's almost three years old now) is to name the shape and then eat it. You and your child both have the same food so if they get stuck, try "monkey see monkey do": "Watch me eat the circle egg. Can Ian eat a circle egg?" And so on. You can also work on colors with this quick and easy lunch. It works great as picnic food or a playgroup snack/lunch. Of course, you can finish with shaped sugar cookies! Suggested reading: *The Color Kittens* by Margaret Wise Brown, Illustrated by Alice & Martin Provensen.

bagel delightful

Circle sandwiches!

Ingredients & Utensils

- 1 cinnamon bagel
- cream cheese
- nuts *(almonds or walnuts work well.)*
- cinnamon sugar
- thin apple slices

"This is a great sandwich! I like cinnamon crunch bagels, but you can use any flavor you like. Try different stuff in them. It is cool."

Directions:

Okay, if your bagel is not already sliced, have your grown–up slice it. Then, with your kid-friendly plastic knife, spread the cream cheese on the bottom and the top. You do both so the middle stuff sticks together (or you can eat it like an open-face sandwich if your mouth is too small). Next, sprinkle your cinnamon sugar or honey on and then add nuts and apple slices. Put the top on and eat. Wow, how many food groups do we have in just one dish?

This is a good time to talk about eating and why we eat different foods to stay healthy. Max was confused over the diet craze of protein-only diets. I showed him the food pyramid and talked about all the ways we can eat a variety of foods. Someone told him that protein was meat. Meat is one source of protein, but we are vegetarians—so I needed to show Max that protein is more than hotdogs, chicken nuggets, and steak. Vegetarians get their protein from nuts, beans, whole grains, tofu, eggs and dairy products. This was also a way for my kids to try new foods that fit into the pyramid. Suggested reading: *The Very Hungry Caterpillar* by Eric Carle.

Mom's tips

crunchy bugs and cheese
Improved Mac and Cheese Dinner.

Max Says:

"Tastes good...
really! Boys, keep
this a secret and
make it for your
sister so she'll
scream. Little
brothers like this
one a lot."

Ingredients & Utensils

- 1 box of Crazy Bugs Macaroni & Cheese by Back to Nature found in the green or organic section of your market.
- 1/4 cup low-fat milk
- 1 tbsp. butter
- 1/2 cup of shredded mild cheddar cheese
- 1/2 cup of cheese sauce
- 1/2 cup of peas
- 8 to 10 crushed whole wheat crackers
- olive oil cooking spray
- spoon
- 8-inch square pan

Directions:

You make the mac and cheese as directed on the box. Then you dump it into your sprayed or oiled 8x8 pan and mix in your peas and cheese sauce. Sprinkle your cheese on top and then put the crushed crackers on top of that. Have your grown-up helper put it into the oven (preheated to 350 degrees) for 20 minutes.

Mom's Tips

Have your little chef crush the crackers by putting them in a plastic baggie and rolling them with a rolling pin. This is a great and somewhat sneaky way to get green veggies into a meal. This is always a hit after a "bug theme" day at school or at play. Suggested reading: *Feely Bugs* by David A. Carter or *The Grouchy Ladybug* by Eric Carle.

mountain of nachos

Monday night football munchies or a great easy meal

Max Says:

Ingredients & Utensils

- 1 16-oz. bag of blue corn tortilla chips or regular corn chips
- 1 8-oz. package of shredded cheddar cheese or an 8-oz. brick of cheddar cheese to grate by yourself. *(Save half of the cheese for the top.)*
- 1 can of crushed tomatoes with green chilies
- 1 can of sliced olives
- 1 small red onion diced
- 1 Roma tomato, diced
- 1 can of black beans, drained
- 1 small lime
- Cookie sheet
- Aluminum foil

Optional add-ons: diced green pepper, cilantro, and jalapeños for my dad.

"It is a whole meal by itself! Having a good nacho meal will give you big muscles and big power to play all day."

Directions:

Cover the cookie sheet with aluminum foil. This makes cleaning up really easy. Now, put a layer of chips on the cookie sheet. Then sprinkle cheese and plop black beans on top along with the onion.

For the next layer, put more chips on top and repeat with the cheese, beans, onion, olives, and the crushed tomatoes with green chilies. *(You can't put the crushed tomatoes or olives on the first layer because that would make the chips mushy.)* Keep repeating the layers until you have a mountain of nachos.

Top it all off with cheese and have your grown-up helper put it in the oven (preheated to 350 degrees) for 20 minutes or until the cheese is all melty. Take out of the oven and let sit for 5 minutes. Dice the Roma tomato and put on top and squeeze lime juice all over it. Bring to the table and serve with mild salsa and sour cream.

Nachos are fun to build together. However, take them out of the oven in a kid free kitchen. It can be awkward taking hot Nachos out of the oven. Suggested reading: *Walter the Farting Dog* by William Kotzwinkle and Glenn Murray, Illustrated by Audrey Coleman. Lot of beans.

Mom's tips

the king's veggies

King Arthur probably ate food this good.

Ingredients & Utensils 🍴

- 1 can of whole potatoes
- 1 can of carrots
- 3 Roma tomatoes quartered
- 1 red onion cut into thick slices
- 12 fresh green beans
  or 8 pieces of broccoli crowns
- olive oil spray
- seasoned salt
- 3 or 4 sprigs of fresh rosemary
- baking sheet
- large bowl

Max Says:

"This feels like a medieval meal, a healthy food for knights in any castle."

Directions:

First, drain your cans of veggies. Then arrange all the veggies on the baking sheet so they don't touch and spray them with the olive oil spray. Now that your veggies are sticky with oil, you can sprinkle them with seasoned salt. We find the best way for kids to do this is by putting the salt in their palm and letting them take pinches of it with one hand to sprinkle it over their cooking. You don't want too much salt in one spot. Next, pull the green leaves of half of the rosemary sprigs and sprinkle that over your veggies. Have your grown-up helper put this into the oven *(preheated to 350 degrees)* and bake for 20 to 25 minutes. Once the potatoes look roasted and golden, they're done. Use a spatula to put them in a bowl, with the other half of the fresh rosemary on top, to look cool. It is called garnish and is a great way to jazz up a dish.

Mom's tips

Now, you can use fresh veggies but you will need to steam them ahead of time. Suggested reading: *The Knight at Dawn* by Mary Pope Osborne. A great chapter book series.

snow people

It is an inside snowman.

Max Says:

"It's okay to eat this snow."

Ingredients & Utensils

- large marshmallows
- mini-marshmallows
- sugar glue *(made with 1/2 cup of powdered sugar and 1 teaspoon of water)*
- decorations — edible color markers, colored frosting, whole cloves, mini M&M's, fruit roll-ups *(for hair and scarves)*, and pretzels and candy *(for hats)*
- toothpicks (or bamboo skewers.)

Directions:

Build your snow person by painting on your sugar glue. We sometimes use the toothpicks or skewers to hold them together until the "glue" dries. Next, put on your fruit roll-up hair and scarf. You won't need more "glue" because it's already sticky. Then put on your snow person's face and buttons. Pretty cute!

You can make them into long lasting ornaments buy using Elmer's Glue instead of sugar glue. Then use cloves as buttons and eyes to help dry the marshmallow. You use markers after the marshmallows have had a day or two to dry out and dress them in yarn and fabric scraps. Mini marshmallows make cute babies wrapped in fruit roll-ups. Suggested reading: *The Snowman* by Raymond Briggs or *A Stranger in the Woods* by Carl R. Sams II & Jean Stoick.

Mom's tips

snow pie

A chilled no bake winter pie.

"We don't have snow here in Georgia, but this "snow" tastes good. And it's easy to make too!"

Ingredients & Utensils

- 1 ready-made pie crust (*we use a graham cracker or cookie pie crust.*)
- 1 large packet of vanilla pudding
- 1 cup of shredded coconut (*the cook might not use it all, but have it just in case.*)

Directions:

The "pie" is the pudding, so make it according to the directions on the box. My mom lets me shake the pudding up in a sealed tight container by jumping up and down for two minutes. Now, two minutes is a long time. So if you get tired, you can always whisk it (that's a fancy word for stirring fast) until it's smooth. Then put it in the refrigerator for five minutes.

When it's chilled, spoon it into the pie crust. Once you do that, take your coconut and make it snow on the pie. Some of the coconut will sink in but keep doing it until you have a layer of snow on top. Put it back into the fridge for at least two hours. Then eat it!

Mom's tips

Serve with snow people on the side and a cup of hot chocolate. Max's aunt is allergic to coconut, so we make our snow pies with a small dusting of mini-marshmallow and powdered sugar snow. While enjoying this tasty treat, talk with your kids about the different seasons. What will happen when winter comes? Suggested reading: *The Mitten* by Jan Brett.

s'mores on a stick

Don't have a campfire? No problem.

Max Says:

"Hey kids,
frozen S'mores
are messy
and fun."

Ingredients & Utensils

- chocolate pudding mix – small package
- 2 cups milk
- 1 cup Cool Whip
- 20 to 30 mini-marshmallows
- 1 graham cracker per cup
- paper cups (3-oz. or 5-oz.)
- wooden sticks for as many cups as you want to make

Directions:

Start by making the pudding as directed on the box. Break up two graham crackers and mix them in and then add some mini-marshmallows and stir them in, too. Next, spoon the mixture into paper cups and add half of a graham cracker sticking out. Put the stick in the middle. Freeze overnight.

Before serving, your frozen S'mores need to sit on the counter a few minutes. Place S'mores on a Stick on the counter for a few minutes before you pull them out of the cup. While enjoying this tasty treat, talk about when you went camping as a kid. Remember any campfire songs? With little kids, try reading *Curious George Goes Camping* by H. A. Rey. Suggested reading: *Bailey Goes Camping* by Kevin Henkes.

Mom's tips

mud cake
Fun and messy.

Max Says:

"Cool!
There's a worm
in *my* cake!
(Put gummy
worms in the
middle with the
cocoa frosting.)"

Ingredients & Utensils

- marble cake mix *(enough to make two 9-inch cakes)*
- 1 small package instant chocolate pudding mix
- 1 8-oz. container of heavy whipping cream
- 1 packet of hot cocoa mix
- 1 gallon-size plastic ziplock bag

Directions:

Prepare cake mix according to directions on the box. Make the pudding per the directions on the pudding box, place in a one-gallon sized ziplock bag, and put in the refrigerator to cool. Now make my special frosting by putting the whipping cream in a bowl with one packet of hot cocoa mix, and beat with an electric mixer until fluffy (if you're too young to use an electric mixer, just watch as your grown-up helper does it for you). By the way, if you beat it too much? You'll end up making chocolate butter. Ick!

Apply the frosting to the top of one cake. Put on gummy worms if you want! Then place the other cake on top. Before serving, take your plastic bag of brown chocolate pudding, cut off one bottom corner of the bag, and "ooze" the mud all over the top of the cake!

Mom's tips

Let the kids read the directions on the cake box. Even if it's just the pictures. As you can imagine, this is a fun birthday cake. Suggested reading: *Diary of a Worm* by Doreen Cronin, Illustrated by Harry Bliss. *(For the gummy worms in the middle.)*

max's favorite dessert

5 minutes to make. Tastes like cheesecake.

> "It has some healthy stuff and some not. It's all good, though."

Ingredients & Utensils

- 1 pint of strawberries *(wash them but leave the green things on.)*
- 8 oz. of brown sugar
- 4 oz. of sour cream
- 1 large plate

Directions:

Get a fancy plate and place a ring of strawberries around the edge. Next, dump the brown sugar in the middle to make a mountain. Then make a crater in the middle of the sugar and dump in the sour cream. Serve right away. Tell people to first dip the strawberries in the cream and then sugar and then eat!

This is a super-fast dessert to make and it looks impressive! Great for company. For the best presentation, put the plumpest strawberry on top of the sour cream. And for an extra taste sensation, sprinkle with cinnamon. Suggested reading: *Olivia Forms a Band* by Ian Falconer. (They eat strawberries at a picnic.)

Mom's tips

marshmallow candy

Good for gift giving.

"I made this after we read *Willy Wonka and the Chocolate Factory.*"

Ingredients & Utensils

- 20 big marshmallows
- 1 cup of sprinkles
- 1 cup of nuts *(your choice.)*
- 1 cup of broken pretzels
- ½ cup milk chocolate chips
- microwave-safe cup
- wax paper
- cookie sheet

Directions:

Place the chocolate chips in the cup and have your grown-up helper microwave them on high for 30 seconds. Take them out, stir them, and then microwave for ten more seconds if they weren't all melted. Next, dip your marshmallow in the melted chocolate and then into one or two of your other dips (sprinkles, nuts, or pretzels). My brother likes sprinkles and walnuts. Set the marshmallow chocolate side down on the wax paper and let cool. If you're in a hurry and can't wait, you can cool them faster in the refrigerator.

Mom's tips

If you're going to cool the treats in the refrigerator, put them on wax paper on a cookie sheet. To present the Marshmallow Candy as a gift, make a fancy candy box and use paper muffin cups as your candy holders. As Max did, read or watch *Willy Wonka and the Chocolate Factory* by Roald Dahl. The biggest and easiest tip is to invent. Almost everything chocolate is good! Suggested reading: *Curious George Goes to a Chocolate Factory* by Margaret & H.A. Rey.

extremely wicked ice cream

You don't have to be a Ben or a Jerry to do this.

Ingredients & Utensils

- ½ gallon vanilla ice cream
- 1 or 2 bananas
- chocolate chips *(as many as you want!)*
- 6 Oreo cookies
- handful of M&M's
- 1 spoon *(a strong one, either wood or metal.)*
- 1 large mixing bowl
- 1 airtight container

Max Says:

"Hey kids! Like some ice cream that tastes great and that's easy to make? Have a blast!"

Directions:

Leave the ice cream on the counter until it's a little bit melty. When it's pretty soft, you can mush it up more with a metal spoon or a strong wooden spoon. Smash the cookies in a plastic bag until you can't see any of the white filling stuff anymore. Next, mix in the bananas, chocolate chips, and smashed cookies. Scoop your creation into an airtight container. Put it in the freezer and leave it there overnight. You thought ice cream was good? Wait until you taste this!

Mom's Tips

inside-out ice cream sandwich

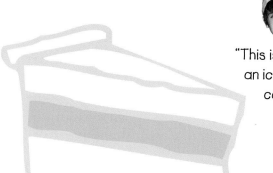

Max Says:

"This is actually an ice cream cake!"

Summertime dessert.

Ingredients & Utensils

- ½ gallon of ice cream *(Your favorite flavor.)*
- 1 small brownie mix *(not the family size.)*
- 1 bread loaf pan *(8 in. or 9 in. is OK.)*
- wooden spoon
- wire rack

Directions:

First make your brownie mix like it says on the package. Cook for the lesser of the times listed *(for example, if it says to bake them for 8 to 12 minutes, you bake them for 8 minutes).* Let your brownies cool before taking them out of the loaf pan and then let them rest on a wire rack. Now rinse the loaf pan and smoosh in a layer of ice cream. Use a wooden spoon to even it out. Now put the brownies back in the pan for the middle of your ice cream sandwich. Perfect fit, right? Then spread the rest of the ice cream over the brownie. Put the whole thing back in the freezer for at least an hour. When you're ready to eat, cut it horizontally and serve with sprinkles.

Mom's tips

We use this fun dessert on a special "Opposite Day". We talk about inside out and outside in. We play match the opposites. I say FRONT and my child says BACK. I say BIG and my child says LITTLE. You can even use two different ice creams on TOP and BOTTOM like CHOCOLATE and VANILLA. Suggested reading: *The Usborne Children's Encyclopedia* by Jane Elliott and Colin King

A Meal with Max

Hey kids, now that you can cook, why not put together a meal? Here are my suggestions, but you can create your own, too. We have a lot of good combinations in this book.

• breakfast •

Tie-Dyed Pancakes with Extra Eggs. I put out a bowl of berries or bananas to put on top of the pancakes. Ask your guest if they want juice or milk to drink.

Or Breakfast Sunday with a Kid's Chocolate Baguette. You can make up some Afternoon Tea but you would drink it in the morning.

• lunch •

Pizza Soup with breadsticks and grapes. Why not have Spritzers to drink and Marshmallow Candy and hot chocolate for dessert?

Bagel Sandwich and Oh, Yeah! Fruit Salad make a great combination, too. A Super Sport Slushy for your drink would be cool, or maybe Georgia Lemonade.

• dinner •

Pirate Pasta is great with Even Better Biscuits. Use Spritzers for your drink and Max's Favorite Dessert to end your meal.

Mountain of Nachos followed by Extremely Wicked Ice Cream is really good.

How about Crunchy Bugs with King Arthur Roasted Vegetables and Thanksgiving Cranberries? Make it really special by having Mud Cake for dessert.

Preview of Max's Next Book

Thanks for cooking with me!

If you have a good recipe, tell me about it at www.CookingWithMax.com. I'll email you one of my new recipes. And hey, I am working on my second book called *Snacks with Max*. It has a whole month's worth of healthy after-school snacks and some weekend treats kids can make.   If I use your recipe in the book, I'll send you a prize!

Max

P.S. Remember good food should be fun and kind of messy.

After School Smoothie

A Good-For-You Treat

Stuff you will need:

blender

8 oz. vanilla low-fat yogurt

1/2 cup pineapple, frozen or canned

5 big fresh strawberries

Ok, you get home and you head for the blender. Have your grown-up helper set it up.

Then you hit the buttons. My blender has a liquefy button—it is loud and cool. In ten

seconds you have a good-for-you after school snack that tastes great.

Makes 2 servings so I can share with my brother, Ian.

Max says
"If you had a bad day at school, add a shot of whipped cream and rainbow sprinkles to the top to cheer you up."

Where is your food from?

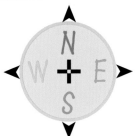

Never Eat Soggy Waffles
to remember
North, East, South, and West.

Metric Conversion Chart by Volume

Standard		Metric
1/4 cup	=	60 milliliters
1/2 cup	=	120 milliliters
1 cup	=	230 milliliters
1 1/4 cups	=	300 milliliters
1 1/2 cups	=	360 milliliters
2 cups	=	460 milliliters
2 1/2 cups	=	600 milliliters
3 cups	=	700 milliliters
4 cups (1 quart)	=	.95 liter
1.06 quarts	=	1 liter
4 quarts (1 gallon)	=	3.8 liters

Metric Conversion Chart by Weight

Standard		Metric
1/4 ounce	=	7 grams
1/2 ounce	=	14 grams
1 ounce	=	28 grams
1 1/4 ounces	=	35 grams
1 1/2 ounces	=	40 grams
2 1/2 ounces	=	70 grams
4 ounces	=	112 grams
5 ounces	=	140 grams
8 ounces	=	228 grams
10 ounces	=	280 grams
15 ounces	=	425 grams
16 ounces (1 pound)	=	454 grams

Metric Conversion Chart by Volume

Metric		Standard
50 milliliters	=	.21 cup
100 milliliters	=	.42 cup
150 milliliters	=	.63 cup
200 milliliters	=	.84 cup
250 milliliters	=	1.06 cup
1 liter	=	1.05 quarts

Metric Conversion Chart by Weight

Metric		Standard
1 gram	=	.035 ounce
50 grams	=	1.75 ounces
100 grams	=	3.5 ounces
250 grams	=	8.75 ounces
500 grams	=	1.1 pounds

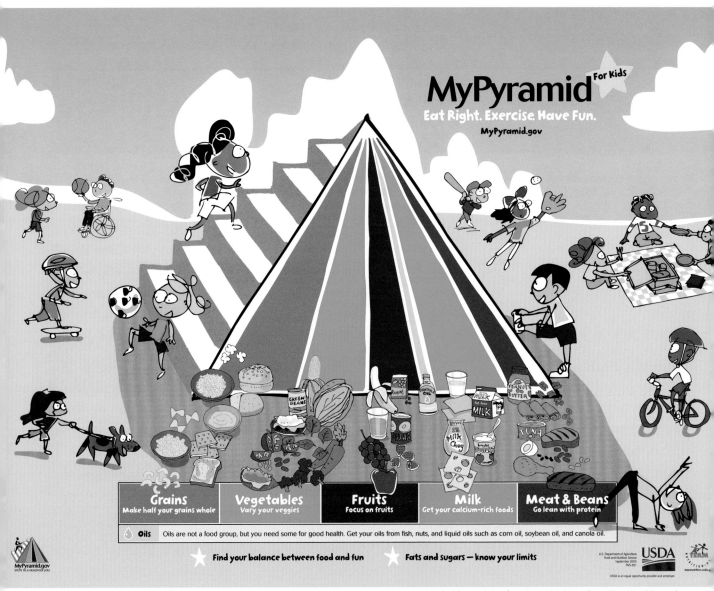

www.CookingWithMax.com

Max's Family

Pictured left to right: Ian, Sienna, Max and John

Now it's your turn

Recipes invented by you and inspired by Max.

Name of little chef: ....

Title of recipe: ....

Ingredients:

1. ....   6. ....

2. ....   7. ....

3. ....   8. ....

4. ....   9. ....

5. ....   10. ....

Instructions: ....

....

....

....

....

....

....

Now it's your turn
Recipes invented by you and inspired by Max.

Name of little chef: ....

Title of recipe: ....

Ingredients:

1. ....   6. ....

2. ....   7. ....

3. ....   8. ....

4. ....   9. ....

5. ....   10. ....

Instructions: ....

....

....

....

....

....

....

....

....

Now it's your turn

Recipes invented by you and inspired by Max.

Name of little chef: ....

Title of recipe: ....

Ingredients:

1. ....   6. ....

2. ....   7. ....

3. ....   8. ....

4. ....   9. ....

5. ....   10. ....

Instructions: ....

....

....

....

....

....

....

Book Order Form

www.CookingWithMax.com

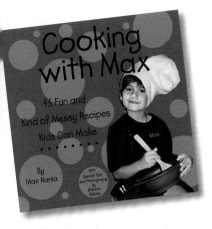

One book is $14.95. Order 2 or more and get free shipping.* Order 4 or more and receive 10% off plus free shipping.* Shipping and Handling: $5.00 for the first book and $1.00 for each additional book.

*Ground shipping only. Allow 1 to 2 weeks for delivery.

❏ Yes, please send me a Five Star Publications catalog.

How were you referred to Five Star Publications?

❏ Friend ❏ Internet ❏ Book Show ❏ Other

Method of payment

❏ VISA ❏ Master Card ❏ Discover Card ❏ AMEX

_____

account number

_____

expiration date

_____

signature

_____

name

_____

address

_____

city, state, zip

_____

daytime phone   fax

_____

email

Item	Qty	Unit Price	Total Price

Mail or Fax your order to:
Five Star Publications, Inc.,
P.O. Box 6698
Chandler, AZ 85246-6698
Fax: 480-940-8787
Phone: 480-940-8182
Toll Free: 866-471-0777

Subtotal	
Shipping	
I bought 2 or more –ship it to me FREE!	
TOTAL	

About Five Star Publications

Cooking with Max is published by Little Five Star, a division of Five Star Publications. Little Five Star's mission is to help authors create books that will help children understand the implications of their life choices and help them become more tolerant and accepting of the differences in others.

President Linda F. Radke, who started the firm in 1985, has worked with hundreds of authors over the years, some famous, some obscure, but all with messages they wanted others to hear. She's garnered a long list of publishing awards along the way. Five Star is one of the country's leading small press publishers, offering consulting, book production, publishing, and full marketing services. Linda was recently named "Book Marketer of the Year" by Book Publicists of Southern California.

Five Star Publications, Inc.,
P.O. Box 6698
Chandler, AZ 85246-6698
Fax: 480-940-8787
Phone: 480-940-8182
Toll Free: 866-471-0777
www.fivestarpublications.com